Preface

Throughout centuries the most disputed book has been the Bible. Some have banned and ridiculed this book. The Bible has even been burned by others . In history kings have stopped its distribution and classified it as illegal. Every terrible act imaginable has been done to the Bible, yet it stands as a guide book to life that is full of truth and prophesies. There is only wisdom and life in this book. Blessings and Curses have been outlined in the Bible and upon them " The Greatest Case of Identity Theft Ever", was written.

I The History of God's Chosen People

*T*he true history of God's chosen people is about to be revealed. Let it be known that The Most High loves us all yet He had a covenant with a certain group of people; the children of Israel. Genesis Ch. 9 is an excellent place to begin our journey to truth and righteousness.

Genesis 9:18

18. And the sons of Noah that went out of the ark were Shem, Ham, and Japheth. And Ham was the father of Canaan.

19. These were the sons of Noah and from these the whole earth was populated.

The later verses show us a conflict between Noah and one of his sons. When Noah began to farm he planted a vineyard and drank of the wine one night and became drunk. While he lay in his tent uncovered, Ham (the father of Canaan) saw his nakedness and went and told his brothers. When Shem and Japheth entered the tent they went in backwards with a garment to cover their father. They kept their faces turned and never saw the nakedness of their father. When Noah awoke from the wine he had known what his younger son had done. This is only the beginning so don't jump to conclusions for the story has not even begun yet.

Genesis 9:24-27

.24 And Noah awoke from his wine, and knew what his younger son had done unto him.

25. Then he said "cursed be Canaan; a servant of servants he shall be to his brethren."

26. And he said: "Blessed be The Lord, the God of Shem, and may Canaan be his servant.

27. May God enlarge Japheth, and may he dwell in the tents of Shem; and may Canaan be his servant.

   These scriptures show that Ham made a mistake and had his seed cursed for it. We also notice from the text that Shem was favored and Noah even wanted Japheths seed to dwell in the tents of Shem.

   One of the biggest misconceptions I have heard from European Christians is that Noah's curse caused his grandson to turn dark skinned. Now the curse fell upon Ham's son Canaan which was already dark skinned already just like his Father Ham. Ham in Hebrew means black or burnt.

Genesis Chapter 11 tells us the whole earth was one language and it gives a rundown of the blood line of Shem starting at verse 10. In the 29th verse we see the familiar name of Abram (later changed to Abraham) and the lady he took to be his wife Sarai(later changed to Sarah).

The first two chapters in twelve shows us that God told Abram to get the out they country and I will make you a great nation. An obedient servant always does as told and he did. Moving along to the fifteenth chapter something very peculiar and prophetic happened. In a dream God spoke to Abram about His seed and some things to come in the future.

Genesis 15:13-14

13. And he said unto Abram, Know of a surety that thy seed shall be a stranger in a land that is not theirs, and shall serve them; four hundred years;

.14 And also that nation, whom they shall serve, will I judge: and afterward shall they come out with great substance.

Now take note of these verses and please remember that number, 400 years. Now moving along to the seventeenth chapter we see that The Lord changed Abram name to Abraham and Sarai to Sarah. God also established a covenant with them giving them all the land of Canaan for an everlasting possession. The scripture further shows us that Abraham was the father of Isaac and Isaac the father of Jacob. Jacob had twelve sons which formed the twelve tribes of Israel and they are as follow: Reuben, Simeon, Levi, Judah, Zebulon, Issachar, Dan, Gad, Asher, Naphtali, Joseph, and Benjamin.

These are the blessed children of Israel which were a part of the covenant made by their forefathers.

Joseph one of Jacobs sons had a Devine dream in the thirty seventh chapter of Genesis. His brothers became extremely jealous and began to plot on Joseph. One day when their father had sent them out his brothers thought of slaying him but Judah decided it would be best to sell him to the Ishmaelite's for twenty pieces of silver. Joseph was then sold into slavery unto Potiphar, and officer of Pharaoh's, and captain of the guard.

Even when cast into slavery the world could see the favor in Joseph.

Genesis 39: 2-4

2. And The Lord was with Joseph, and he was a prosperous man; and he was in the house of his master the Egyptian.

3. And his master saw that The Lord was with him, and that the Lord made all that he did prosper in his hand.

4. And Joseph found grace in his sight, and he served him: and he made him overseer in his house, and all that he had put into his hand.

The wife of Joseph's master devised a plan to secretly sleep with Joseph when her husband and the other men were out the house but she did not know that Joseph was a honorable man. Joseph , A Hebrew –Israelite refused to sin against God and for this the master's wife began to hate him and plan for his downfall. She had held on to a piece of garment that she had taken from Joseph while trying to convince him to sleep with her. This same piece of garment she used as false evidence when she presented the situation to her husband in verse 14.

Genesis 39:14

That she called unto the men of her house , and spake unto them, saying, See, he hath brought in a Hebrew unto us to mock us; he came in unto me to lie with me, and I cried out with a loud voice.

Even when cast into prison because of the lies and deception of men The Lord was with Joseph. The keeper of the prison saw something special in Joseph and Joseph was given privileges while he was stuck in bondage.

{Gen 39 v. 22-23}.

22. And the keeper of the prison committed to Joseph's handball the prisoners that were in prison; and whatsoever they did there, he was the doer of it.

23. The keeper of the prison looked not to anything that was under his hand; because The Lord was with him, and that which he did, The Lord made it to prosper.

Joseph once interpreted some dreams while in prison, and as usual favor was shown to him. When the king needed an interpretation of a dream he was told about Joseph who was still incarcerated. Upon Joseph revealing what the dream meant to the king, Joseph was then made governor! When God's hand is upon you His hand is simply upon you.

During a famine in the Canaan Jacob sent his sons to Egypt to buy food. Upon this arrival they bowed down to the seller of goods which was now Joseph (governor of Egypt). This was the event that he foresaw and caused his brothers to be greatly angered with him. He recognized them yet they did not recognize him. Let us note that these are a people loved by God in which a covenant was in place. Joseph soon moved all his family to Egypt where they no longer had to do without anything. These are the true people of Israel for Jacob changed his name to Israel after an encounter with an angel.

Joseph had favor with the Pharaoh but when the Pharaoh passed the new king knew nothing of Joseph. Fear that the Hebrews would soon overtake the Egyptians arose from the new king so he began to enslave the Hebrews. This is the first documented case of slavery. Despite being enslaved the more the king afflicted the children of Israel the more they grew. His next solution was that the Hebrew midwives slay all male children and allow only the females to live. The midwives feared the true and living God and could not do as the king commanded. The king then charged all his people demanding that all males be slain.

A Levi lady had a son that she knew she could hide no longer so she placed him in a basket in the river. The child was found by the maidens of the daughter of Pharaoh who realized he was one of the Hebrew children. The child was taken by Pharaoh's daughter and was named Moses because he was drawn out the water. Moses lived in

Pharaoh's house forty years until he was grown. One day Moses could not stand the sight of an Egyptian dealing harshly with a Hebrew and Moses slew him.

In fear of his life Moses fled Egypt. While resting in the land of Midian by a well he encountered seven daughters of the priests that were being hindered by shepherds. Moses helped them and the ladies told their father in chapter 1 of Exodus that they were helped by an Egyptian.

Exodus 1:19

.19 And they said, An Egyptian delivered us out of the hands of shepherds, and also drew water enough for us, and watered the flock.

Note: These ladies could not tell the difference from Moses or the Egyptians because they were all of the same skin tone. The Egyptians were of Noah's son Ham. There was no difference in the appearance of these men as Hollywood has depicted for years.

In chapter three of Exodus we note that while tending to the flock of his father-in-law an Angel appeared to him in a flame in the midst of a burning bush. God firmly let Moses know that He was the God of Abraham, the God of Isaac, and the God of Jacob. Moses was afraid and hid his face.

Chapter 3 of Exodus is very important so brethren open your ears to hear the Words of the true Living God.

Exodus 3:7

7. And The Lord said, I have surely seen the affliction of my people which are in Egypt, and have heard their cry by reason of their taskmasters; for I know their sorrow;

A magnificent relationship it is to be singled out and claimed by the Most High. Moses was instructed to approach the Pharaoh and demand the release of the children of Israel. Hesitantly Moses asked, "who am I to approach the Pharaoh and to bring forth my people the children of Israel out of Egypt". God assured Moses that he would surely be with him. The Lord then let Moses know that He had surely hardened Pharaoh's heart and that he would not initially comply but that He would smite Egypt with all His wonders thereof. Moses was also assured that favor would be granted when they left and jewels of gold and silver would be placed upon the neck of his sons and daughters as they left Egypt.

Despite talking to a burning bush Moses could still not believe the manifestation of Devine intervention. For a sign to Moses and the people, The Lord turned the rod in Moses's hand to a snake and Moses immediately ran. The Most High then told Moses to place his hand into his robe and when he did his hand turned white as snow. These were the signs that Moses would take before the Pharaoh and the children of Israel. God then gave a message to Moses to deliver to the Pharaoh and we can see the love that God has for the children of Israel.

Exodus 4:22-23

22. And thou shall say to Pharaoh, Thus says The Lord, Israel is my son, even my firstborn.

23. And I say unto thee, Let my son go, that he may serve me: and if thou refuse to let him go, behold, I will slay thou son, even thou firstborn.

Let us surely make note of this. That God himself called the children of Israel his son and his firstborn. It is not hard to see the love that The Most High has for these people. Ten Commandments were given to the Children of Israel that God himself issued. These commandments found is Exodus 20 were the only time the Bible recorded instructions so important that God issued and had them placed upon a stone Himself. The Hebrew-Israelites had a special relationship with the Most High and they were considered His first born.

II The Physical appearance of the Hebrews, Ethiopians, and Egyptians

One of the most well-known Biblical movies to date was the Ten Commandments produced by Cecil B. Demille. Charles Heston (a Caucasian male) played Hebrew –born Moses that became the deliverer of his people, the Hebrew slaves of Egypt. This film was one of the most successful films ever financially despite being severely inaccurate. This film was even selected for preservation in the United Stated Film Registry by the Library of Congress in 1999. With all its inaccuracies it was stated as being "culturally, historically, and aesthetically significant ". I find this amazing because the Egyptians and Hebrews were all played by Europeans. A rational mind when it truly pursues to enlighten people about Gods prophetic word would remain as accurate as possible, one would think.

We best return to the scripture of Genesis to get an accurate description of the Hebrews, Egyptians, and

Ethiopians. The ninth chapter and eighteenth verse of Genesis tells us that Noah had three sons; Shem, Ham, and Japheth. Ham had four sons.

- Cush (Ethiopians / Cushites & Nubians).

- Miriam (Egyptians / Khemet).

- Phut (Ancient Libyans or Somolia).

- Canaan (Canaanites—the original inhabitants of Israel)

This genealogy can be traced through the tenth chapter of Genesis the sixth through nineteenth verse.

All of Ham's sons and their descendants settled in or close to the continent of Africa. Ham's sons were people of the African continent, the Ethiopians, Egyptians, Somalians, and Canaanites. Ham in Hebrew means black or burnt so these people being a race of dark people should not be a surprise to us.

The Israelites are the direct descendants of Noah's son Shem. Through Shem Abraham is the father of Isaac, Isaac the father of Jacob, and Jacob's sons composed the twelve tribes of Israel. Each of his sons became a tribal nation that made up the greater nation of Israel.

A simple reading of the scriptures clearly states that all these men resembled in color. For starters, when Hebrew born Joseph took Hebrews and Egyptian servants with him to bury is father Jacob (Israel) in Gen. 50 v. 7-11 a Canaanite saw them

and said, " This is a grievous mourning of the Egyptians". Now this was a mixed entourage of people yet the Canaanite could not distinguish the difference from the two.

In Exodus we saw that Moses –a Hebrew, was born of the tribe of Levi and was discovered in a basket by an Egyptian. Moses was raised as the Pharaoh's grandson and spent forty years in Pharaoh's house according to Acts 7:23. The Pharaoh had issued that all Hebrew males be put to death at this time yet he did not even notice one living in his own house.

Once Moses had fled Egypt for killing an Egyptian, the seven daughters of the priest of Midian could not distinguish him (a Hebrew) from an Egyptian. After a pleasant encounter with Moses they told their father that they had been delivered by an Egyptian {exodus 2:16-19}.

.19. And they said, An Egyptian delivered us out the hand of the shepherds, and also drew water enough for us, and watered the flock. Interesting, as of now no one can tell the difference in the Hebrews or Egyptians.

Two important verses in the New Testament further show us that distinguishing between these groups of people was virtually impossible. The book of Matthew shows us that Joseph (parent of Jesus) was warned in a dream to take their child (Jesus) into Egypt for Herod is seeking the life of the child (St. Matthew ch2:13). Now if Jesus had been white like many

 would want you to believe , why would God go tell them to hide in a country of dark skinned people? I know that makes no sense. Even Paul which wrote thirteen books of the New Testament was mistaken for an Egyptian in the twenty first chapter of Acts, verses 37-39.

.37 And as Paul was led into the castle, he said unto the chief captain, May I speak unto thee? Who said, Canst thou speak Greek?

 38. Art thou that Egyptian, which before these days made an uproar, and leddest out into the wilderness four thousand men that were murders?

39. But Paul said, I am a man which am a Jew of Tarsus, a city on Cilicia, a citizen of no mean city: and, I beseech thee, suffer me to speak unto the people.

The above noted scriptures let us know that that these great men of God were in fact dark skinned people. Hollywood and white supremacist would like for you to think differently. A mass campaign to hide the true identity of these great men of God was begun hundreds of years ago. Many would say that it matters not if they were black or white. I respond with, if it didn't matter, why was scripture left out of the Ten Commandments the movie (and many more publications)? The euphoria of thinking they were a chosen people or maybe it was to hide the fact that another race of people (African-Americans, Dominicans, etc.) we're loved and chosen by God Himself.

Their goal was to convince the general public that these chosen people of God were European.

III. The blessings promised to God's chosen people

From the beginning of time it's a known fact that God loves us all. His unselfish love has been with man since the beginning of time. It's never God that turns his back on us its always us that depart from the Living God first.

One fact that cannot be hidden or denied is the special relationship God had with his chosen people; the children of Israel. We are all blessed to have the Most High with us but fact remains the true Children of Israel have multiple blessings in store. The love relationship between the children of Israel is seen all throughout the bible. It must be addressed so that we can identify and awake the true heirs to these promises God himself said he would bring forth.

Deuteronomy 28:1-14

- And it shall come to pass, if thou shalt hearken diligently unto the voice of The Lord thy God , to observe and to do all his commandments which I command thee this day, that The Lord thy God will set thee on high above all nations of the earth:

- And all these blessings shall come on the, and overtake thee, if thou shalt hearken unto the voice of The Lord thy God.

- Blessed shalt thou be in the city, and blessed shalt thou be in the field.

- Blessed shall be the fruit of thy body, and the fruit of thy ground, and the fruit of thy cattle, the increases of thy kind, and the flocks of thy sheep.

- Blessed shall be thy basket and thy store.

- Blessed shalt thou be when thou comest in, and blessed shalt thou be when thou goest out.

- The Lord shall cause thine enemies that rise up against thee to be smitten before thy face: they shall come against thee one way, and flee before thee seven ways.

- The Lord shall command the blessing upon thy storehouses, and in all that thou set test thine hand unto; and He shall bless thee in the land which The Lord thy God giveth thee.

- The Lord shall establish thee an holy people unto himself, as he hath sworn unto thee, if thou shalt keep the commandments of The Lord thy God, and walk in his ways.

- And all people of the earth shall see that thou art called by the name of The Lord; and they shall be afraid of thee.

- And The Lord shall make thee plenteous in goods, in thy fruit of thy body, and in the fruit of thy cattle, and in the land which The Lord sware unto thy fathers to give thee.

- The Lord shall open unto thee his good treasure, the heaven to give the rain unto thy land in his season, and to bless all the work of thine hand: and thou shalt lend unto many nations, and thou shalt not borrow.

- And The Lord shall make thee the head, and not the tail, and thou shalt be above only, and thou shalt not be beneath; if that thou hearken unto the commandments of The Lord thy God, which I command thee this day, to observe and to do them:

- And thou shalt not go outside from any of the words which I command thee this day, to the right hand, or to the left, to go after other gods to serve them.

God simply asked the children of Israel to keep these commandments. What honor it is to have a personal relationship of love with the creator of mankind. The Most High chose these people to be a light into the dark world. These promises still stand as of today.

Matthew 5:14-17

.14 Ye are the light of the world. A city that is set on a hill cannot be hid.

.15 Neither do men light a candle, and put it under a bushel, but on a candlestick; and it giveth light unto all that are in the house.

.16 Let your light shine before men, that they may see your good works, and glorify your father which is in heaven.

.17 Think not that I am come to destroy the law, or the prophets: I am not come to destroy but to fulfill.

Please never let anyone tell you that the Old Testament is "nailed to the cross". Jesus came to take away the judgment of the law not the law itself. Anytime you hear anyone say otherwise it is my prayer that you present them with the above scriptures.

Note: There are powerful men that know these scriptures well and do not want the true children of Israel to receive any of these blessings listed in this chapter.

Isaiah 49:1-16

- Listen, O isles, unto me; and hearken, ye people, from afar;

  The Lord hath called me from the womb; from the bowels of my mother hath he made mention of my name.

- And he hath made my mouth like a sharp sword; in the shadow of his hand hath he hid me, and made me a polished shaft; in his quiver hath he hid me;

- And said unto me, Thou art my servant, O Israel, in whom I will be glorified.

- Then I said, I have labored in vain, I have spent my strength for nought, and in vain: yet surely my judgement is with the Lord, and my work with God.

- And now, saith The Lord that formed me from the womb to be his servant, to bring Jacob again to him, Though Israel be not gathered, yet shall I be glorious in the eyes of The Lord, and my God shall be my strength.

- And he said, it is a light thing that thou shouldest be my servant rise up the tribes of Jacob, and to restore the preserved of Israel: I will also give thee for a light to the Gentiles, that thou may be my salvation unto the end of the earth.

- Thus saith The Lord, the Redeemer of Israel, and his Holy One, to him whom man despiseth, to him whom the nation abhors, to a servant to rulers, Kings shall see and arise, princes shall also worship, because of The Lord that is faithful, and the Holy one of Israel, and he shall choose thee.

- Thus saith The Lord, In an acceptable time have I heard thee, and in a day of salvation have I helped thee: and I will preserve thee, and give thee for a covenant of the people, to establish the earth, to cause to inherit the desolate heritages;

- That thou mayest say to the prisoners, Go forth; to them that are in darkness, Shew yourselves. They shall feed in the ways, and their pastures shall be in all high places.

- They shall not hunger or thirst; neither shall the heat nor sun smite them: for he that hath mercy on them shall lead them, even by the springs of water shall he guide them.

- And I will make all my mountains a way, and my highways shall be exalted.

- Behold, these shall come from far: and, lo, these from the north and west; and these from the land of Sinim.

- Sing, O heavens; and be joyful, O earth; and break forth into singing, O mountains: for The Lord hath comforted his people, and will have mercy upon his afflicted.

- But Zion said, The Lord hath forsaken me, and my Lord hath forgotten me.

- Can a woman forget her sucking child, that she should not have compassion on the son of her womb? Yea, they may forget, yet will I not forget thee.

- Behold, I have graven thee upon the palms of my hands; thy walls are continually before me.

A covenant and a declaration of love from The Creator is unprecedented. Many have attended traditional services their entire life without knowing the declarations of Love and Promise that God made for his chosen people.

Be not mistaken every declaration from The Most High is for everlasting. These blessings shall fall upon the chosen ones on earth and in heaven. What the Most High loves He loves.

Revelation 21:10-12

10. And he carried me away in the spirit to a great and high mountain, and showed me that great city, the holy Jerusalem, descending out of heaven from God,

11. Having the glory of God: and her light was like unto a stone most precious, even like a jasper stone, clear as crystal;

12. And a wall great and high, and had twelve gates, and at the gates twelve angles, and names written

thereon, which are the names of the twelve tribes of the children of Israel:

The names of the twelve tribes of Israel are to be written on the gates of Heaven. These children of Israel were destined to be blessed in heaven and on earth. No greater promise was made to any other group of people than this.

IV The warning of the curses.

God Himself warned the children of Israel of curses that would fall upon them and all their generations if they were not obedient. These curses are outlined in Deuteronomy 28 and Leviticus 26. It is clearly evident that the African –Americans are one of the cultures of people that these plagues fall upon. My friends you are about to be simultaneously amazed at saddened about what these scriptures are about to reveal to you.

The warning from God was clearly placed in Deuteronomy .

Deuteronomy 28:15

15. But it shall come to pass, if thou wilt not hearken unto the voice of The Lord thy God, to observe to do all his commandments and his statutes, which I command thee this day; that all these curses shall come upon thee, and overtake thee.

Now this was the warning label the Israelites paid no attention to.

Deuteronomy 28: 68

.68 And The Lord shall bring thee into Egypt (slavery) again with ships, by the way where of I spake unto thee, Thou shalt see it no more again: and there ye shall be sold unto your enemies for bondsmen and bond women, and no man shall buy you.

Throughout the bible Egypt is commonly referred to as a condition of slavery. Egypt was the first documented place of slavery in the Bible. The Lord used Moses to inform the Israelites that they would see the Egyptians no more before God parted the Red Sea for Moses and his people in Exodus 14:13.

Now let it be known, the so called African-Americans were surely taken from their land by ships and placed into slavery. We were taken on a journey that God said we would never see again. It was even told to Abraham in Genesis.

Genesis 15:13

.13 And he said to Abram, Know of a surety that thy seed shall be a stranger in a land that is not theirs, and shall serve them; and they shall afflict them 400 years;

We all know that African Americans were brought here by ships and served as slaves in a strange land (USA) for 400 years. I wanted to establish this curse first so that any rational thinking person can easily identify who these curses fell upon. Deuteronomy Verse 26 states;

26. Your carcasses will be food for all the birds and wild animals, and there will be no one to frighten them away.

During the notorious "middle passage" where slaves were brought to America millions of slaves died and were thrown overboard. So many slaves perished on this journey that it was said that sharks began to follow the ships. As a matter of fact even in America blacks were mutilated, hung, shot , stabbed , and their carcasses were left in woods or even put on display. Don't be amazed so far we are just beginning to scratch the surface.

The 28th verse of Deuteronomy may explain to us why they are spiritually drunk, and a confused race of people to this date.

.28 The Lord will afflict you with madness, blindness, and confusion of mind:

How many times have you thought to yourself what is wrong with the so called African-American people? Sadly African Americans even have a record as having seven times the rate of mental illnesses or disorders as our white counter parts.

Even down to the financial oppression that African Americans suffer to this date Is mentioned in the 29th verse

Deuteronomy 28:29

.29 At midday you will grope about like a blind person in the dark, You will be unsuccessful in everything you do; day after day you will be oppressed and robbed , with no one to rescue you. Despite being in this strange land longer than anyone else besides their colonial slave owners and the native Indians they are less productive than any other culture. In urban neighborhoods all across the country the corner stores and gas stations are owned by foreigners as opposed to blacks. It is very doubtful that you could go to a neighborhood in India, Sudan, or anywhere else and find a black owned business in their neighborhood. Only in the African American neighborhoods will you see this and this was specifically foretold as well in the 43rd and 44th verse.

Deuteronomy 28:43-44

.43 The foreigners who reside among you will rise above higher and higher, but you will sink lower and lower.

44. They will lend to you, but you will not lend to them. They will be the head, but you will be the tail. By now there should be no doubt in one's mind who God is referring to and that they are from one of the twelve tribes of Israel.

Deuteronomy 28: 45-49

45. All these curses will come upon you. They will pursue you and overtake you because you did not obey The Lord your God and observe the commandments and decrees he gave you.

46. They will be a sign and a wonder to you and your descendants forever.

47. Because you did not observe The Lord your God joyfully and gladly in the time of prosperity, Therefore in hunger and thirst, in nakedness and dire poverty, you

will serve the enemies The Lord sends against you. He will put an iron yoke on your neck until he has destroyed you.

49. The Lord will bring a nation against you from far away, from the ends of the earth, like an eagle swooping down, a nation whose language you will not understand.

The above listed curses were brought about because the children of Israel simply did not keep God's commandments as quoted in verse 45. Simple obedience was the key to survival so these plagues continue to haunt our people. The conditions of our ancestors in slavery immediately came to mind the first time I read the 48th verse. Pay special attention to the end of the scripture where God says, "He will put an iron yoke on your neck until he has destroyed you". When slaves were in transport an iron yoke was worn around their neck so that they could not run or escape. Today they wear an invisible yoke that was imbedded in us from years of psychological abuse. Centuries of being severely mistreated has done much damage to African Americans (the true Hebrew Israelites). That iron yoke placed on them centuries ago led to the rape, murder, torture, and

humiliation of their ancestors. The 49th verse was frighteningly prophetic and gives us further evidence that African Americans are a part of the true children of Israel. It specifically mentions that an enemy will come from far away (colonial slave owners). It also mentions that they will come like an eagle swooping down and it will be a nation whose language we will not understand. The bald eagle is the national symbol of the United States of America and you can all rest assured that they did not understand their language when we were first placed in captivity.

Leviticus 26: 23-25

.23 And if you will not be reformed by me by these things, but will walk contrary unto me;

24. Then will I also walk contrary unto you, and will punish you seven times for your sins.

25. And I will bring a sword upon you that shall avenge the quarrel of my covenant: and when you are gathered together in your cities, I will send pestilence among you; and you shall be delivered into the hands of your enemies.

I didn't come to overwhelm you with statistics but it is common knowledge that the turmoil and distress of the African American communities is at a constant rise. Despite being a minority our people make up the majority of street gangs. Their children would not behave as such if they understood they have royal blood running through their veins. Bullets fly through their neighborhoods and strike those that are completely innocent. The foolishness of confused men and women are destroying them at an alarming rate. When the blood has been shed in the streets, then the perpetrators of the crimes are "delivered into the hands of their enemies" , as verse 25 states. The confusion amongst them is heartbreaking and they commonly end up in jails and prisons.   (Isaiah 42: 22)

22. But this a people robbed and spoiled; they are all of them snared in holes, and they are hid in prison houses: they are for a prey, and none delivereth; for spoil, and none smith, Restore.

African Americans suffer the highest incarceration rates among all races of people. They have surly been caught

in snares and hid away in prisons. The lack of unity among them is unprecedented.

Leviticus 26: 36-37

.36 And upon them that are left alive of you I will send a faintness of heart in the land of their enemies; and the sound of a shaken leaf shall chase the and they shall flee, as a fleeing from a sword, and they shall fall when none pursue the.

.37 And they shall fall one upon another, as it were before a sword, when none pursue the: and ye shall have no power to stand before your enemies.

The years of oppression of the African Americans have left them in a state of depression and confusion. They constantly look for answers for what makes their lives complicated and have had the answers to their questions right before their eyes. They are the true descendants of the Hebrew Israelites and they still suffer these curses. It is imperative they awaken so that they can rebuild and be the productive people that God intended for them to be. They must reconnect with The Most High.

Romans 11:7-8

7. What then? Israel hath not obtained that which he seeketh for; but the election hath obtained it, and the rest were blinded

8. (According as it is written, God hath given them the spirit of slumber, eyes that they should not see, and ears that they should not hear;) unto this day.

V   The Diaspora

I would like to give the readers a definition of the word **Diaspora** before I began this chapter. This definition is from the Merrim-Webster dictionary.

- Capitalized

A. The setting of scattered colonies of Jews outside Palestine after Babylonian exile

B. The area outside Palestine settled by Jews

C. The Jews living outside Palestine or modern Israel

2.

A. The movement, migration, or scattering of a people away from an established ancestral homeland < the black diaspora to northern cities>.

B. people settled away from their ancestral homeland <African Diaspors>

C. The place where these people live.

Where are the Israelites today? To help us get a clear understanding lets go to the words of The Most High.

Jeremiah 24:8-9

.8 And as the evil figs, which cannot be eaten, they are so evil; surely thus saith The Lord, So will I give Zedekiah the king of Judah, and his princes, and the residue of Jerusalem, that remain in this land, and them that dwell in the land of Egypt:

9. And I will deliver them to be removed into all the kingdoms of the earth for their hurt, to be a reproach and a proverb, a taunt and a curse, in all places whither I shall drive them.

Deuteronomy 28:62-64

.62 And ye shall be left few in number, whereas ye were as the stars in Heaven for multitude; because thou wouldest not obey the voice of The Lord thy God.

.63 And it shall come to pass, that as The Lord rejoiced over you to do you good , and multiply you; so The Lord will rejoice over you to destroy you, and to bring you to

nought; and you shall be plucked from off the land whither thou goest to posses it.

.64 And The Lord shall scatter thee among all people, from one end of the earth even unto the other; and there thou shalt serve other gods, which neither thou nor thy fathers known, even wood and stone.

Through the mouth of the prophet Jeremiah and from the words of The Most High, the children of Israel shall be scattered all over the earth. Although it is difficult to track their every move there is some account of the lands they migrated to.

Historians recorded Israelites in Tamentil, " The Israelite Town ", in as early as 5AD. They were a skilled group of people that was prosperous. Most of them were said to be land owners and farmers that lived peacefully. The Nomads recognized their abilities and grew jealous of their wealth. In 1492 they were attacked by the Nomads and most of the Israelites were killed.

Cyrene, Libya 125 AD

The Israelites escaped Roman persecution in Jerusalem after the Roman-Jewish war and then moved to Libya.

There hopes were to establish a Hebrew empire there but the Romans stopped them once again. This forced them to further into Africa.

Two centuries after being exiled from Jerusalem some Israelites established themselves In Yemen. This group of Israelites later migrated to Timbuktu in Africa which was the center of civilization at the time. Ze el Yemeni came from these Israelites and was the founder of the old Kingdom of Ghana and the Za Dynasty, which was a dynasty of Israelite Kings.

They were another group of prosperous people that followed the law of Moses not the Talmud. Around the 600's Muslims began to dominate the area which led to the Saharan Trade through Ghana. By 1000 AD it is said the Israelite kings converted to Islam (and their people followed) for financial gain and to be In agreement with Islamic traders.

It was around the 1441 when the Portuguese began to traffic slaves. Arab Muslims were said to have informed them where the Hebrew Israelites (so called Africans) dwelled in West Africa. The first load of the Trans Atlantic trade was said to have begun in the early 1500's and was to Hispaniola (present day Dominican Republic & Haiti).

Between 1650-1850 millions of slaves had been transported through the Trans Atlantic routes from western Africa. Many historians record millions being shipped to America, but there were even more shipped to the West Indies, Central America, and South America.

The following were regions where slave ships docked and unloaded slaves:

South America (SA)   North America (NA)

Recife (SA)- One of the first areas in Brazil to be settled by the Portuguese Crown.

Salvador (SA)- now known as Brazil's capital of happiness

Buenos Aires (SA)- the capital and largest city in Argentina

Lima (SA)- capital of the republic of Peru

Valparaiso (SA)- the capital of Chile

Paramaribo (SA)- the capital and largest city of Suriname,

West Indies- "The Caribbean" comprised of more than 700 islands on the Caribbean Sea

Mexico City (NA)- founded by the Aztecs in 1321

Europe- by convention one of the world seven continents; comprised of Spain, UK, France, Italy, Germany, Switzerland, Belgium, Ukraine

New Orleans (NA)-major US port & the largest city in Louisiana

Charleston(NA)- oldest and second largest city in the southeastern state of South Carolina

Richmond(NA)- the capital of the commonwealth of Virgina

These are just a minute description of the regions where the true children of Israel reside today. The scripture surly tells us that they will be scattered all over the Earth.

Leviticus 26:33

.33 And I will scatter you among the heathen, and will draw out a sword after you: and your land shall be desolate, and your cities waste.

VI   Who are the Khazars?

The people that occupy Israel right now are from the Aryan Turk tribes what is known as the "Khazarian Empire". They were originally in Turkey but was driven out because of their ruthlessness about 500 AD. A few of them migrated to Romania and Turkey and became gypsies.

Aryan; White race, speakers of Indo-European languages such as Greek, Celtic, Armenian, French, and Spanish.

Turk; The people residing In Siberian (Russian) area.

The Khazarians were born Gentiles not Jews and they are the sons of Noah's son Japheth.

Genesis 10:1-5

- Now these are the generations of the sons of Noah, Shem, Ham, and Japheth: and unto them were sons born after the flood.

- The sons of Japheth; Gomer, and Magog, and Madai, and Javan, and Tubal, and Meshec, and Tiras.

- And the sons of Gomer; Ashkenaz,Riphath, and Togarmah.

- And the sons of Javan ; Elishah, and Tarshish, Kittim, and Dodanim.

- By these were the Gentiles divided in their lands; every one after his tongue, after their families, in their nations.

  The Jews who reside in Israel today once lived in Khazarian Empire. They populated from the Black Sea to Caspian and from the Caucasus area to Volgsa. This is where white people came from. Have you ever thought about where the name "Caucasian "came from? They got the name because they came from the Caucasus Mountains.

In the 700-800's King Bulan the Khazarian could not decide which religion he wanted himself and his people to partake in. The king sent and had representatives of Christianity, Islam, and Judaism brought before him. He asked all the men one simple question. If one day they decided to convert to another religion, which would it be? The Muslim and and the Christian both said Judaism so the King now had direction. In 740 AD king Bulan of Khazarian chooses to convert to the beliefs of Moses and he made all his people convert as well. In the upcoming generations there was several attempts to overthrow the Judaic Khazarian Emperor . The Vikings tried in 965 AD and the Kipchak in 1000 AD. It wasn't till the 1200's AD that the Mongolian

King Genghis Khan overthrew the Khazarians and threw them off of their land.

The Khazars migrated from the Caucasus Mountains through Ukraine, Poland , and Central Europe in the 1300's but were persecuted everywhere they went. There was no documentation of their history and they never knew that they were not the true Israelites but only converts to the Israelite beliefs. Completely ignorant of their history they traveled through Europe carrying the name of a cursed group of people. The following is a small list of plaques that the Khazarians (Israelite Imposters) fell upon.

- " Christian Crusades Massacre Jews" (1096)

- " Jews Massacred in England" (1190)

- " Jews burned at Troyes" (1288)

- " Jews expelled from England" (1290)

- " Jews expelled from France" (1306)

- " Thousands of Jews Massacred In Europe

  (Black Death) "1347

- "Jews expelled from Spain " 1492

- " Horrible Persecution of Jews in Germany (1st Holocaust)" 1630

- " Jews persecuted in Russia by Nicholas I " 1829

- " first set of Jews to migrate to Israel" 1882

- " Jews expelled from Moscow" 1891

- " second wave of Jews to migrate to Israel" 1903

- " third wave of Jews to migrate to Israel" 1918

- "Holocaust, six million Jews slaughtered" 1939

The true Israelites were enduring harsh persecutions as well through Yemen and Africa because of their refusal to convert to Islam or Christianity. They traveled all over Africa to be free of persecutions. The Islamic Arabs eventually enslaved them in West Africa and advertised them as "yahoo dee"; meaning "the tribes of Israel ".

In the 1500's the real Hebrew Israelites were being taken onto boats and brought to a strange land fulfilling the prophesies of Deuteronomy that we discussed earlier.

Deuteronomy 28:68

68. And The Lord will bring you into Egypt again with ships, by the way whereof I spake unto thee, Thou shalt see it no more again: and there ye shall be sold unto your enemies for bondsmen and bond women, and no man shall buy you.

Note: I would just like the readers to remember that Egypt is frequently mentioned in the scripture when it pertains to "a condition of slavery". It was in Egypt where slavery first began. Also know that anything from the 2nd Century forward written about Jews is written about the Khazarian converts not the true Jews, the children of Israel. The Khazarians did an excellent job of assuming the identity of the original Hebrew Israelites. They also suffered some of the curses that true Hebrew Israelites were enduring.

Hitler did not know these were not the true "Jews ", and that they were not chosen by God. He hated them with a passion yet he never knew they were operating

under a "false title". Hitler and his soldiers used harsh inhumane methods to kill millions of theses Khazarian converts.

In 1948 the Khazars fled to Israel in great numbers. They had convinced themselves they were the true Jews and that Israel was where they should dwell.

Please reflect upon the national emblem which was chose by these Jewish converts to symbolize their nation. The "star of David" as many would call it , yet it is better known as "the star of moloch". Moloch was a pagan god that even Solomon began to seek after.

Acts 7:43

Yea , ye took up the tabernacle of Moloch, and the star of your god Remphan, figures which you made to worship them: and I will carry you away beyond Babylon.

This hexagram which is the national emblem of Israel today has a dark history. Hexagrams are frequently used in the occult to summon demons. The terminology of "putting a hex" on someone even

derived from this word. People of the Most High do not carry this symbol.

In Genesis we noted that these Khazarians were descendants of Noah's son Japheth and that they were born Gentiles chapter 10 verses 1-5. Men can change and cover-up whatever they like but they cannot hide the truth forever. The Word of God is truly sharper than any two edge sword. The word even exposes these Imposters in Revelations .

Revelations 2:9

9. I know thy works, and tribulation, and poverty,(but thou art rich) and I know the blasphemy of them which say they are Jews, and are not, but they are the synagogue of Satan.

Can the Word of God say it any clearer? Years ago one of my mentors told me that God will always tell you something twice; and He did then. The Most High does it once more for His true Children. In Revelations 3:9 He confirms that which He originally spoke.

.9 Behold, I will make them of the synagogue of Satan, which say they are Jews, and are not, but do lie;

behold, I will make them to come and worship before thy feet, and to know that I have loved thee.

If these Khazarian converts had have known of the curses to fall upon the true children of Israel they may have not been so steadfast in claiming our heritage. At any capacity the prophesies had to be fulfilled, right down unto Revelations.

Isaiah 1:3

The ox knoweth his owner, and the ass his master's crib: but Israel doth not know, my people do not consider.

2 Thessalonians 2: 8-12

8. And then shall the wicked be revealed, whom The Lord shall consume with the spirit of his mouth, and shall destroy with the brightness of his coming.

9. Even him, whose coming is after the working of Satan with all power and signs and lying wonders,

10. And with all deceivableness of unrighteousness in them that perish; because they received not the love of the truth, that they might be saved.

10. And with all deceivableness of unrighteousness in them that perish; because they received not the love of the truth, that they might be saved.

11. And for this cause God shall send them strong delusion, that they may believe a lie:

12. That they all might be damned who believe not the truth, but had pleasure in unrighteousness.

The book of Revelations paints the picture clear about these Khazarian people living in Israel right now. Now these people were once called the "serpent people" and we all know the serpent represents. When the Most High speaks, we need to listen!

VII Jews, Muslims, and the so called African slave trade.

For decades many have called the evil of slavery the African slave trade. History records it as such because the Israelites that were taken into bondage were living in Africa. The only reason they resided there was because they had been scattered abroad seeking peace and fleeing from the persecution of the Romans.

Peace was found in Africa but it was not everlasting. During the rise of Islam the Arab Muslims along with black converts were the first to organize and implement the so called-African slave trade. It was these followers of Muhammed's Islam that enslaved many and sold them to the European Judaist converts. It has been documented that the Arab Muslims may have been involved in slavery 1100 years before the European Judaist converts even began.

Note: I call these Europeans converts because that is what they are –converts. Let me give you the true definition of – Jew.

Jew; a member of the tribe of Judah

The Messiah (Jesus Christ) was a true Jew.

How many times in the scriptures can you recall Him being called "The King of Jews"?

The enslaved Israelites were deemed less than men and women even though their tormentors knew who they were. The Arab Muslims told the Portuguese their location in Africa and told them they were called Yahoodee, " The Tribes of Israel". The Hamitic Curse mentioned in chapter one was the justification used to sooth their souls about enslaving the Hebrew Israelites. Perhaps it made it easier for them to justify mistreating these people if they believed they were already cursed and sub human. They did not care or know that these people were the descendants of Noah's son Shem not Ham.

Genesis 9: 24-26

24. And Noah awoke from his wine, and knew what his younger son had done unto him.

25. And he said, Cursed be Canaan; a servant of servants shall he be unto his brethren.

26. And he said, Blessed be The Lord God of Shem; and Canaan shall be his servant.

   The Portuguese began shipping slaves to the Caribbean's as well as North and Central America as early as 1441. This was beginning of what was called the Trans-Atlantic slave trade.

Hispaniola was one of their very first locations. This area now consists of the sovern nations of the Dominican Republic and Haiti.

Aaron Lopez (1731-1782) was just one of the many Jews that made the slave industry a lucrative business for himself. Lopez was born in Lisbon, Portugal .He later moved to the American colonies and managed several businesses; slavery being his primary. A book called "The Secret Relationship Between Blacks and Jews", described Lopez as "Newports leading participants in the Black Holocaust". By the 1770's Lopez was the wealthiest person in Newport. The growing tension between Britain and America made his slave trade earnings decline. When the British landed on Newports harbor in 1775 the city began to evacuate and Lopez relocated. He is just one of the many that used slavery for financial gain.

Jews also were extremely lucrative in other areas such as the providers of chains and restraints that would bind the slaves so they could not escape. The business of slavery had corporation structure and easily turned a profit because it provided almost free labor to the already wealthy slave owners. Money over morals was the principle that anyone in this business lived by.

There is a term associated with modern so called African American Muslims that have converted to the beliefs of their former Arab enslavers. Stockholm syndrome is a group of

psychological symptoms that occur in people that have been held captive before. Stockholm allows hostages to sympathize with their captors. It is of my opinion that that is what has happened with American Muslims.

The American Muslims have either been deceived or suffer serious psychological disorders to even want to identify with those that sold their ancestors into slavery. What would make a person want to convert to the beliefs of their oppressors? Any African American considering Muslim conversion could just as easily consider converting to any faith of the European. The Europeans were involved in the trafficking of flesh far fewer years than the Arab Muslims.

This is common knowledge that can be found anywhere only if a person reads. With reference to only one movie "Malcolm X" I would like to ask the readers three questions. What did Malcolm X really find out when he went to Mecca? What information was he warned not to speak of? Why was Malcolm X assassinated? Find the answers and you will know that the movement was not that of God but that of men.

There is also a term associated with the Judist converts that to this day try and claim a heritage under false pretense. The term is called identity theft and let me define it for you.

Wikipedia: Identity Theft

Identity theft is a form of stealing someone's identity in which someone pretends to be someone else by assuming that person's identity, typically in order to access resources or obtain credit and or other benefits in that person's name.

Let's not forget these are the same people in the previous chapter that once were a part of the Khazarian Empire. They can convert to anything they want but they cannot inherit the blessings of God's chosen people. The blessings of Deuteronmy 28:1-14 belong to the true Hebrew Israelites. These Judaist converts are the people mentioned in Revelations 2:9 and 3:9

Revelations 2:9

9. I know thy works, and tribulations, and poverty, (but thou art rich) and I know the blasphemy of those that say

they are Jews, and are not, but you are the synagogue of Satan.

Revelations 3:9

.9 Behold, I will make them of the synagogue of Satan, which say they are Jews, and are not, but do lie; behold, I will make them come to worship before thy feet, and to know that I have loved thee.

In Revelations 2:9 we can see that the Most High knew that these people would be rich. God knew the earthily wealth they sought after. Earthly wealth cannot obtain you a seat in heaven

nor can you deceive the Most High. Our Father already knows how the story will end.

More prophetic facts:

The following is a direct quote from WEH Lecky , A History of England in the Eighteenth Century, Volume IV, Chapter 5(1878)

The greatest period of the English slave trade had, however, not yet arrived. It was only in 1713 that it began to attain its full dimensions. One of the most important and most popular parts of the Treaty of Utrecht was the contract known as the Assiento, by which the British Government secured for its subjects during thirty years an absolute monopoly of the supply of slaves to the Spanish Colonies. The traffic was regulated by a long and elaborate treaty, guarding among other things against any possible scandal to the Roman Catholic religion from the presence of heretical slave-traders, and it provided that in thirty years from 1713 to 1743 the English should bring into the Spanish West Indies no less than 144,000 negroes, or 4,800 very year, that during the first twenty-five years of the contract they might import a still greater number on paying certain moderate duties, and that they might carry the slave trade into numerous Spanish ports from which it had hitherto been excluded.

The first time I read this contract the number 144,000 immediately caught my attention. It reminded me of a couple

of prophetic verses in Revelations. The promise given to the children in Israel are clear and present in this Devine revelation of Heaven as well.

Revelation 7:4

.4 And I heard a number of them which were sealed: and there were sealed an hundred and forty and four thousands of all the tribes of the children of Israel.

There are millions of combinations of number that are dealt with in contracts. The contractual mention of the 144,000 in my eyes lets us know that prophecy is simply being fulfilled. The true children of Israel will have their names written in Heaven along with the Apostles that walked with the Messiah.

Revelations 21:12

.12 And had a wall great and high, and had twelve gates, and at the gates, and at the gates twelve Angles, and names of the twelve tribes of the children of Israel:

VIII   A Nation Asleep

The majority of the Hebrew Israelite nation as of date is completely asleep. There are many of us that have seen the light yet our numbers are few in comparison with the millions of unknowing. A variety of methods were used to blind these chosen of God. The false doctrine that the has infiltrated Christianity is greatly to blame . We were already a people that was robbed of their culture and taken away to a land whose language we did not understand. Perhaps our enemies feel that the longer we are kept in darkness the longer we will continue to struggle and the longer they continue their rule.

Being systematically targeted and victims of centuries of psychological abuse the so called –African Americans not only suffer from an identity crisis they also have not learned to unite amongst each other. They are a royal chosen people that was blessed by God and was asked only keep His commandments. Being ignorant of their special relationship with The Most High, the majority of them still worship Pagan traditions in the name of Christ. The Roman Catholic Church took it upon itself to change the Sabbath to intentionally deny the world a True relationship with The Most High.

Quote from the Catholic Record

"Sunday is our mark of authority... the Church is above the Bible, and this transference of Sabbath observance is proff of fact"- The Catholic Record, London, Ontario, September 1, 1923

What arrogance it takes of a man to boast that his church is above the Bible. It truly hurts to be delivered out of darkness and realize that you have spent years in an institution that has lied to to and deceived you from the start. It is much easier to say this manuscript is a lie and that its writers know not what they are talking about. We came simply to restore a nation of lost people back to the original state of The Most High so that they can receive the true blessings they were promised in Heaven and on Earth. There is no material in this book that cannot by googled and confirmed. Remember our adversary is extremely good at what he does, so get over it, move on, and claim what has been rightfully yours from this day forth. Even by the reading this material and you have begun to awake out of darkness.

Sadly many may choose to deny the truth and rely on the righteousness of their former slave owners and their present day motivational speakers (pastors) that do not give them the full word of The Most High. It is imperative that they wake out of this slumber for they have a covenant and a special judgment before the Most High.

Genesis 17: 19-21

.19 And God said, Sarah thy wife shall bear thee a son indeed; and thou shalt call his name Issac: and I will establish my covenant with him for an everlasting covenant , and with his seed after him.

.20 And as for Ishmael, I have heard thee: Behold, I have blessed him, and I will make him fruitful, and I will multiply him exceedingly; twelve princes he shall begat, and I will make him a great nation.

.21 But my covenant I will establish with Issac, which Sarah shall bear unto thee at this time in the next year.

Matthew 19:28-30

.28 And Jesus said unto them, Verily I say unto you, That ye which have followed me, in the regeneration when the Son of Man shall sit in the throne of his glory, he also shall sit upon twelve thrones, judging the twelve tribes of Israel.

.29 And every one that hath forsaken houses, or brethren, or sisters, or father, or mother, or wife, or children, or lands, for my James's sake, shall receive an hundredfold, and shall inherit everlasting life.

.30 But many that are first shall be last; and the last shall be first.

    We know that Abraham was the father of Issac, Issac the father of Jacob, and Jacob(Israel) the father of the twelve tribes of Israel. This is who the covenant was established with and it still stands of today. It is the wish of many that we do not awaken and remain in our oppressed state.

As you just read the children of Israel have a special judgment even in Heaven. The twelve Apostles will sit on thrones and judge the twelve tribes of Israel as the scripture states. The Most High loves the children of Israel and will make them great in the Kingdom of Heaven. There are some exceedingly wicked men that know this and have done a wonderful job at suppressing the truth about the blessings in store for these chosen ones. If this is your first time hearing this I strongly urge you to consult with your pastor after reading this book. His response to you will let you know if you are in True Christianity or involved in a church that practices just the business of Christianity.

I have witnessed the so called-African American suffer many plagues that hindered their people and could not understand what was happening. I've watched community leaders have meeting after meeting to no avail.

Deuteronomy 28:28

.28 The Lord shall smite thee with madness, and blindness, and astonishment of heart:

The incarceration rates of the so called- African Americans have soared throughout the years and this is no coincidence, this is what was meant to be until they simply wake up!

Isaiah 42:22

.22 But this is a people robbed and spoiled; they are all of them snared in holes, and they are hid in prison house: they are for a prey, and none delivereth; for a spoil, and none saith, Restore.

How many more must perish before they simply awake and return to the natural order of God. We have allowed paganism to be inserted into Christianity and either many do not know or do not care. People have become robots that follow the best motivational speaker as opposed to the Word of the Most High.

Our pastors that know the truth and have held it back from you will be held accountable. How ignorant can any man or woman be to think they escape the judgment of The Most High?

I just now came into the knowledge of how Satan has infiltrated Christianity. Now that we know better must lead our family away from the traditions of men. We owe it to our children's children to end the foolishness of Satan the moment we are aware of his devices.

The enemy does his job well, and long ago he implemented satanic rituals into Christianity. Many do not know how Easter and the December 25th celebration of Christmas came about.

Noah's son Ham had a son named Cush. Cush married a woman named Semiramis. They were the King and Queen of Babylon. The two had a son named Nimrod. Upon the death of Cush Semiramis married her own son Nimrod. That's right, she married her own son. Nimrod was an excellent warrior and hunter but was extremely rebellious against God. When Nimrod was killed his enemies chopped his body up to prove he was not a God. His wife (mother) recovered all of his body except his penis. Semiramis believed he ascended to the sun making him a sun god. He then became being known as Baal, and was glorified. Constatine the Roman Emperor worshipped the sun god on Sunday and influenced the changing of the sabbath from Saturday to Sunday. Semiramis changed her name to Ishtar, then to Easter.

She pronounced the moon to be a fertility God and claimed that she descended from the moon on an egg. Then she claimed she landed in the Euphrates after the equinox during the first full moon. This egg became known as "Easter's Egg". Nimrod was a great hunter this the reason for the Easter egg hunt. She (Easter) later gets pregnant and claims that the sun rays from her dead husband impregnated her. Easter then gave birth to a son which was named Tammuz. Tammuz was extremely fond of rabbits; which began the "Easter Bunny". He was later killed by a wild animal and his blood spilled all over a tree stump. His mother claimed the tree mysteriously grew overnight and the Evergreen tree became the symbol of the

rebirth of Tammuz. Every year people began to cut down evergreens and decorate them. This is the beginning of the Christmas tree. Infant babies were sacrificed in the name of Easter and the babies blood was used to paint the eggs in hopes that they would hatch nine months later on December 25th .This is the reasons for the painting of Easter eggs and for the December 25th worship of Christmas.

Two pagan worship days were disguised and slipped right into Christianity. The worship of the moon goddess was disguised as a celebration of the risen Messiah and the rebirth of Tammuz was disguised as the birth of the Messiah.

Jeremiah 10:2-4

.2 Thus saith The Lord, Learn not the way of the heathen, and be not dismayed at the signs of Heaven; for the heathen are dismayed at them.

.3 For the customs of people are vain: for one cutteth a tree out of the forest, the work of the hands of the workman, with the axe.

4. They deck it with silver and with gold; they fasten it with nails and with hammers, that it move not.

Matthew 15:9

.9 But in vain do they worship me, teaching for doctrines of the commandments of men.

In Matthew 15:9 we see that Jesus is not pleased with us following the doctrines of men. He clearly states in this verse, "in vain do they worship me". Is this really how we want Jesus to see our service toward Him?

No matter what faith you claim it is a must that you properly do your research. The true Hebrew Israelites were stripped of their culture and their names so it's hard to connect to roots that you know nothing of. Sadly our ancestors did not have the freedoms we had and were forced to adapt to the religions of their colonial slave owners. It wasn't even to the late 1700's when the so called African-American we're even allowed to have the altered version of Christianity. Anyone that aims at the oppression of any people cannot be relied on to present the truth about anything. If goodness and mercy were in them they would not have allowed the ancestors of the true Hebrew Israelites help build this country for free.

By no means are those of the African American communities the only ones asleep; they have more brothers and sisters than they can imagine.

The Brazilians, Dominicans, Guatemalans, Panimanians, Argentinians, Chileans, Mexicans, Aztecs , Jamaicans, Cubans, Purto Ricans, Haitians, and Latinos have also been traced back to the twelve tribes of Israel as well.

IX What about the Messiah?

Several prophets had prophesied about the coming of the Messiah in the Old and New Testament. I will leave off any theory which I may have and only refer to the Word of God on an issue important as this one. The prophets Isaiah, Nathan,

Micah, and Jeremiah all gave accounts of the Messiah that was to come.

Isaiah 9:6-7

6. For unto us a child is born, unto us a son is given: and the government shall be upon his shoulder: and his name shall be Wonderful, Counselor, The mighty God , The everlasting Father, The Prince of Peace.

7. Of the increase of his government and peace there shall be no end, upon the throne of David, and upon his kingdom, to order it, and to establish it with judgment and with justice from henceforth even forever. The zeal of The Lord of hosts will perform this.

Isaiah 11: 10-12

.10 And in that day there shall be a root of Jesse, which shall stand for an ensign of the people; to it the Gentiles shall seek: and his rest shall be glorious.

.11 And it shall come to pass in that day , that The Lord shall set his hand again the second time to recover the remnant of his people, which shall be left from , from Assyria, and from Egypt, and from Pathros, and from Cush, and from Elam, and from Shinar, and from Hamath, and from the islands of the sea.

12. And he shall be an ensign for the nations, and shall assemble the outcasts of Israel, and gather together the dispersed of Judah from the four corners of the earth.

   Note: The Merriam-Webster dictionary documents the Middle English usage of ENSIGN as meaning a banner, sign, or token.

Isaiah 53:3-12

3. He is despised and rejected of men; a man of sorrows, and acquainted with grief; and we hid as it were our faces from him; he was despised, and we esteemed him not.

4. Surely he hath borne our grief's, and carried our sorrows: yet we did esteem Him stricken, smitten of God, and afflicted.

5. But he was wounded of our transgressions, he was bruised for our iniquities: the chastisement of our peace was upon him; and with his stripes we are healed.

6. All we like sheep have gone astray; we have turned everyone to his own way; and The Lord hath laid on him the iniquity of us all.

7. He was oppressed, and he was afflicted, yet he opened not his mouth: he is brought as a lamb to the slaughter, and a sheep before her sneerers is dumb, so he open eth not his mouth.

8. He was taken from prison and from judgment: and who shall declare his generation? For he was cut off out of the land of the living: for the transgression of my people was he stricken.

9. And he made his grave with the wicked and with the rich in his death; because he had done no violence, neither was any deceit In his mouth.

10.Yet it pleased The Lord to bruise him; he hath put him to grief: when thou shalt make his soul a offering for sin, he shall see his seed, he shall prolong his days, and the pleasure of The Lord shall prosper in his hand..

11. He shall see the travail of his soul, and shall be satisfied: by his knowledge shall my righteous servant justify many; for he shall bear their iniquities.

12. Therefore will I divide him a portion with the great, and he shall divide the spoil with the strong, because he hath poured out his soul unto death: and he was numbered with the transgressor; and he bare the sin of many, and made intercession for the transgressors.

The book of Isaiah alone gives us more than enough scripture to conclude that the Messiah mentioned is our Lord and Savior Jesus Christ. Micah even specifically prophesies about the birthplace of the Messiah to come.

Micah 5:2

.2 But thou, Beth-Lehman Ephratah, though thou be little amongst thousands of Judah, yet out of thee shall he come forth unto me that is to be ruler in Israel; whose going forth have been from old, from everlasting.

In the 1st Chronicles 17th chapter the prophet Nathan is talking with David and it confirms what is previously stated.

11. And it shall come to pass, when thy days be expired that though must go to be with thy fathers, that I will raise up thy seed after thee, which shall be of thy sons ; and I will establish his kingdom.

.12 He shall build me a house, and I will establish his throne forever.

13. I will be his father, and he shall be my son: and I will not take away my mercy from him, as I took it from him that was before thee:

Throughout the years we have all heard that the Old Testament is just that, old. The Most high did not perform signs and wonders to just have them forgotten when the Messiah came. The one thing a man of God revealed to me is that the Most High will always tell you twice so let me apply the scriptures of the above prophets to the New Testament.

Note: The above prophets gave their revelations almost 800 years before the New Testament.

The Messiah manifests in the flesh.

St. Matthew 1:1

1. The book of the generation of Jesus Christ, the son of David, the son of Abraham.

Old Testament Confirmation [Micah 5:2] [Isaiah 11:2] [1 Chronicles 17:11]

The Messiah was sent to bare our sins.

1 Peter Ch.1 v. 24

.24 Who his one self bare our sins in his own body on the tree, that we, being dead to sins, should live unto righteousness: by whose stripes ye were healed.

Old Testament Confirmation [Isaiah 53:5]

The Most High knew that the Messiah would be afflicted.

St. Matthew 26:39

.39 And he went a little further, and fell on his face, and prayed, saying, O my farther, if it be possible, let this cup pass from me: nevertheless not as I will , but as thou wilt.

Old Testament Confirmation [Isaiah 53:5]

The Messiah was non- violent and without sin.

Hebrew 4:15

.15 For we have not an high priest which cannot be touched with the feeling of our infirmities; but was I. all points tempted like as we are, yet without sin.

Old Testament Confirmation [Isaiah 53:9]

The Messiah justified many yet was a suffering servant. He was rejected of men and crucified.

St. Matthew 20:28

.28 Even as the Son of man came not to be ministered unto, but to minister, and to give his life a ransom for many.

Old Testament Confirmation [Isaiah 53:11]

The Messiah was called by many names.

Philippians 2 :9-11

.9 Wherefore God also hath highly exalted him, and given him a name which is above every name:

10. That the name of Jesus every knee should bow, of things in heaven, and things in earth, and things under the earth;

11. And that every tongue should confess that Jesus Christ is Lord, to the glory of God the Father.

Old Testament Confirmation [Isaiah 9:6]

The Messiah will be a sign or token to his people:

St. Matthew 15:24

But he answered and said, I am not sent but unto the lost sheep of the house of Israel.

Old Testament Confirmation [Isaiah 11:10]

Just as we have just seen the Old Testament to confirm the New, Jesus came to confirm the law not to abolish it. He is the carrier of the new covenant, and judgment of the law has now been replaced with Grace. The law still stands. Anyone who tells you differently is mistaken and cannot be relying upon scriptures for the Word of God says:

St. Matthew5:17-19

17. Think not that I cone to destroy the law, or the prophets: I am not come to destroy, but to fulfill.

18. For verily I say unto you, Till heaven and earth pass, one jot or one title in no wise pass from the law, till it all be fulfilled.

19.Whoever therefore shall break one of these least commandments, and shall teach men so, he shall be called the least in the kingdom of heaven: but whosoever shall do and teach them, the same shall be called great in the kingdom of heaven.

This is the Word of God. It saddens me that many pastors have spoken contrarily in the past and as of now. Let us not be ignorant that because an individual carries a title it does make them a true vessel. Many churches operate as businesses and have completely been misled from being the body of Christ.

The Messiah came to save all those who had faith but there was a special covenant and a special judgment for the true children of Israel. This covenant begins in the 17th chapter of Genesis verse 7 and is mentioned dozens

of times throughout the Bible . The special judgment and blessings were even given to John on the island as The Most High spoke with him.

Revelations 7:3-4

.3 Saying, Hurt not the earth, neither the sea, nor the trees, till we have sealed the servants of our God in their foreheads.

4. And I heard a number of them which were sealed: and there were sealed an hundred and forty and four thousands of all the tribes of the children of Israel.

The true Hebrew Israelites (not the converts that are in Israel now) have their names written on the gates of pearl in Heaven. They are a chosen and loved people by the Most High.

Revelations 21:12

.12 And had a wall great and high, and had twelve gates, and at the gates twelve angles, and names written therein, which are the names of the twelve tribes of the children of Israel:

To The Most High Be The Glory!

X   Where do we go from here?

It is vital that we return to the original state of God so that we may inherit the blessings promised to us. False prophets have intentionally steered us away from the simplicity that lies in the Most High. Many have been lead to believe the Old Testament is "nailed to the cross"; scripture tells us differently.

St. Matthew 5:18-19

18. For verily I say unto you, Till heaven and earth pass, one jot or one title shall in no wise pass from the law, till all be fulfilled.

19. Whosoever there shall break one of these least commandments, and shall teach men so, he shall be called least in the kingdom of heaven: but whosoever shall do and teach them, the same shall be called great in the kingdom of heaven.

I could give my personal opinions all day long but The Word of God is what it is; the truth. The Ten Commandments were put in place for a reason, we must thoroughly obey them. These words were given directly from the Most High in Exodus and let us revisit this chapter so that we gain a clear understanding of what we are called to obey. [Exodus 20: 3-17] Summary

- Thou shalt have no other Gods before me.

- Thou shalt not make unto the any graven images.

- Thou shalt not take the name of The Lord in vain.

- Remember the Sabbath day, to keep it Holy.

- Honor thy father and thy mother.

- Thou shalt not kill.

- Thou shalt not commit adultery.

- Thou shalt not steal.

- Thou shalt not bear false witnesses against thy neighbor.

- Thou shalt not covet.

Somewhere we have gotten away from the basic things that The Most High asked of us. Wikipedia records thousands of denominations of the Christian faith yet we have only one heaven. The doctrine of men has been imbedded in us as opposed to the doctrine of God. [Isaiah 3:12]

.12 As for my people, children are their oppressors, and women rule over them. O my people, they which lead thee cause thee to err, and destroy the way of thy paths.

How many famous so called leaders have even covered the material mentioned in this book? I count all men who are in the authoritative positions to speak out, yet they do not. They will be held responsible for prolonging Kingdom work. Sadly even many of our religious leaders are concentrating on motivational speaking as opposed to the true deliverance of The Word. I do not consider it harsh to label many of these as performers that fascinate themselves in the doctrine of

men. Closely examine the material that these individuals present for your salvation is on the line. [Matthew 7:22-23]

22. Many will say to me in that day, Lord, Lord, have we not prophesied in thy name? and in thy name have cast out devils? And in thy name done wonderful works?

23. And then will I profess u to them, I never knew you: depart from me, ye that work iniquity.

Many Pastors and performers have simply gotten away from the natural order that The Most High intended for us to receive. They may possibly feel the congregation would be bored or not as fascinated if they preached the simplicity of Christ week after week. Motivational speakers have lead many astray and they will be held accountable for their deeds. [Romans 10:1-3]

- Brethren my heart's desire and prayer to God for Israel is, that they might be saved.

- For I bear them record that they have a zeal of God, but not according to knowledge.

- For they being ignorant of God's righteousness, and going about to establish their own righteousness, have not submitted themselves unto the righteousness of God.

The keeping of the commandments cannot be neglected on our journey of restoration to the original

state of God which we are called upon. Revelations 22:14 tells us how important this is.

.14 Blessed are they that do his commandments, that they might have right to the tree of life, and may enter in through the gates into the city.

The first four commandments pertain directly to the Most High. It is reasonable to assume He demands we zealously keep them to obtain the blessing we were promised.

The keeping of the Sabbath is mentioned all throughout the bible but traditional Christians pay it no mind. When is the Sabbath day? Genesis 2:2-3 tells us when the Sabbath actually is.

.2 And on the seventh day God ended his work which he had made; and he rested on the seventh day from all his work which he had made.

.3 And God blessed the seventh day, and sanctified it : because that in it he had rested from all his work which God created and made.

Nowhere in the bible did God make the names of the day, that task fell upon man. When man named the days of the week Saturday was listed as the seventh day.

Encyclopedia Britannica records Saturday as the seventh day of the week.

Merriam-Webster

Sat-ur-day

: the seventh day of the week

Yourdictionary.com

Saturday

: The seventh and last day of the week.

So the question is where did we get Sunday from as the seventh day?

In 321 AD a Roman Emperor by the name of Constantine instructed that Christians and non-Christians be instructed to worship on Sunday. Constantine was allegedly the first Christian Emperor yet he also practiced paganism. He practiced the rituals of sun-worship and wanted the venerable day of the sun(Sunday) to be recognized as their Holy day. This plan was contrary to the each of the first four commandments which pertained directly to service toward the Most High. Constantine's so called conversion to Christianity was really a plot by Satan to bring about a flood of Pagan compromise into the worship of the one True God. A direct insertion of the worship of idols and disobedience to God were both brought about in this shift of the Sabbath.

Even colonial slave traders were told by the Romans that Sunday should be the day that the slaves rested. The Queen assured everyone it was ok to own slaves as long as they were led to Jesus Christ. By the time African Americans slaves were allowed to congregate in the 1700's many slave owners simply used Christianity as a vice to help their slaves suffer peacefully.

Ten small things asked of us by God and to this day the majority of us cannot properly perform all ten. Many simply do not know of the above material. Every device of Satan has been told to us through the Word of God and it will lie upon us to search the scriptures for ourselves to find the truth.

Matthew 15:9

.9 But in vain do they worship me, teaching for doctrines the Ten Commandments of men.

1st Timothy 4:1

- Now the spirit speaks expressly, that in the latter times some shall depart from the faith, giving heed to seducing spirits, and doctrines of devils;

  Time out my friends for complex motivational stories and worshipping idols. We as children of The Most High must learn and rely on the simplicity of Christ. Man attempted to make the purest form of Love complex and not easily understood. We are all one in Christ yet the fact does remain that the true Children of Israel have an additional blessings that awaits them. [Revelation 21:12]

.12 And a wall great and high, and had twelve gates, and at the gates twelve Angles, and names written thereon, which are the names of the the twelve tribes of Israel:

Exodus 31:12-18

.12 And The Lord spake unto Moses saying,

.13 Speak thou also unto the children of Israel, saying, Verily my Sabbaths you shall keep: for it is a sign between me and you throughout your generations; that ye may know that I am The Lord and that I may sanctify you.

.14 Ye shall keep my Sabbath therefore; for it is holy unto you: every one that defile it shall surely be put to death: for whosoever doeth any work therein, that soul shall be cut off from among his people.

.15 Six days may work be done; but in the seventh is the Sabbath of rest, holy to The Lord: whosoever doeth any work in the Sabbath day, he shall surely be put to death.

.16 Wherefore the children of Israel shall keep the Sabbath, to observe the Sabbath throughout their generations, for a perpetual covenant.

.17 It is a sign between me and the children of Israel for ever: for in six days The Lord made heaven and earth, and on the seventh day he rested, and was refreshed.

.18 And he gave unto Moses, when he had made and end communing with him upon mount Sinai, two tables of testimony, tables of stone, written with the finger of God.

Note: As mentioned before Jesus Christ took way the punishment of the law but the law still stands.

The synagogue of Satan wants us to fail. It is my prayers that all can learn the simplicity of Christ. We must return to the natural state of obedience to the Most High and no longer follow the traditions of men. Satanists have even testified that it gives homage to Satan when we don't sanctify the true Sabbath for he was the first to be defiant. Anytime Gods children show disobedience it pleases the enemy. There is no need for any of us to suffer for a lack of knowledge, everything written in this book can be easily

referenced and researched. Many blessings upon my friends and please beware of the traditions of men.

Made in the USA
Columbia, SC
27 February 2024

32361555R00054